My Friend

has
Dyslexia

By Nicola Edwards

Chrysalis Children's Books

First published in the UK in 2004 by
(✒) Chrysalis Children's Books
An imprint of Chrysalis Books Group
The Chrysalis Building, Bramley Road
London W10 6SP

ISBN 1 84458 095 4

British Library Cataloguing in Publication Data for this book is available from the British Library.

Produced by Tall Tree Ltd.

EDITORIAL MANAGER: Joyce Bentley
EDITOR: Jon Richards
DESIGNERS: Ed Simkins and Ben Ruocco
PHOTOGRAPHER: Michael Wicks
PICTURE RESEARCHER: Lorna Ainger
ILLUSTRATIONS: Hardlines Ltd

CONSULTANT: John Rack, Dyslexia Institute
The Dyslexia Institute (DI) is an educational charity that assesses and teaches people with dyslexia and trains specialist teachers. To find out more about them, contact the office listed on page 31.

Read Regular, READ SMALLCAPS and Read Space; European Community Design Registration 2003 and Copyright © Natascha Frensch 2001-2004

This book has been designed using Read Regular™, a dyslexic friendly font. The letters have been individually shaped to make them easily identifiable, the spacing is even to stop words from 'jumping' on the page and the paper has been tinted cream to reduce the contrast of black text on white paper. All these factors help dyslexics to overcome the difficulties that they face.

The author, photographer and publishers would like to thank Rosie Berkshire, Janet Pearson, Prina Patel, Venetia Patel, Preti Patel, Urvashi Patel, Dylan Patel, Pam Davies, Ron Davies, David Schueler and Buckingham College Preparatory School, Pinner, Middlesex, for their help in preparing this book.

PICTURE ACKNOWLEDGMENTS:
Alamy/Ethno/Gregory Stringfield 13, Jim Pickerell 7
Corbis/Dave Bartruff 17b
Getty Images/Express Newspapers 29, Anthony Harvey 27b, Eric Schaal 9b

Printed in China

10 9 8 7 6 5 4 3 2 1

Contents

WORDS IN SMALLCAPS ARE EXPLAINED IN THE GLOSSARY ON PAGE 30.

My friend Rachel

▶ Rachel and Bella are very good friends.

Hi! My name is Bella and this is my best friend Rachel. We've been friends since we started school together and we are in the same class. After school, I often go to Rachel's house or she comes over to mine. We're always dressing up and putting on shows for our parents to watch. Rachel loves deciding what we are going to wear.

I want to be a television presenter when I am older. Rachel says she's going to be a fashion designer. She's really confident about it.

Rachel's changed a lot. When she started at school I thought she was shy and she seemed quiet and sad. Now I know that she was worried that people would laugh at her because she found reading and writing difficult.

Then Rachel found out that she had DYSLEXIA and that this was affecting how she learned to read and write. Now Rachel knows how to deal with her dyslexia and there are lots of things she can do to stop it from being a problem.

▲ Now Rachel knows how to deal with her dyslexia she is much happier and a lot more confident.

DYSLEXIA FACTS

People with Dyslexia

About four in every hundred people are severely dyslexic. Another six people per hundred have mild or moderate dyslexia. More boys than girls have been DIAGNOSED with dyslexia, but girls are just as likely to be affected. Perhaps this is because dyslexia is less noticeable in girls, who may be better at coping with the SYMPTOMS.

Growing up

Rachel and I are choosing photographs of ourselves to make into a big collage. 'Look at me in that photo,' laughs Rachel. 'I'm doing the bum-shuffle! Mum says I didn't crawl at all when I was a baby. I used to sit up and scoot along sideways like a crab!' Rachel likes hearing stories about what she was like as a baby. 'When you were learning to talk,' Rachel's mum remembers, 'You used to mix up your "c" and "g" sounds. You used to say "tat" instead of "cat" and you'd point at a dog and say "dod"'.

'You used to love being read to,' Rachel's mum tells her. 'Yes,' agrees Rachel, 'it was much more fun being read to than trying to read for myself. I remember getting angry one day when you tried to teach me some letters. Did you think then that I might be dyslexic?' 'Not at all,' Rachel's mum told her. 'It was only when you started school that I began to wonder.'

◀ Opposite: Rachel and Bella love looking at photographs of themselves when they were little.

▲ At nursery school, children who are later diagnosed with dyslexia may speak very well but have difficulty learning to write letters.

DYSLEXIA FACTS

The Signs

Some early indications that a pre-school child may later be diagnosed with dyslexia are:

- 'bum-shuffling' rather than crawling
- difficulty learning how to get dressed
- dislike of jigsaw puzzles
- difficulty remembering nursery rhymes
- problems with throwing and catching a ball
- forgetfulness and difficulty following directions, such as up, down, left, right
- a love of stories and being read to, combined with a lack of interest in letters and words

Feeling different

▶ Rachel has a lot of help from our teacher with her reading and writing.

'What made you think that I might be dyslexic, Mum?' asked Rachel. 'Well,' said her mum, 'the main thing was that there seemed to be a big gap between how clever we knew you were and how difficult you were finding reading and writing.'

'I used to get really frustrated at school,' said Rachel. 'I hated feeling that I was different from other people and not as good as everybody else.'

'Also,' said Rachel, 'some of the other kids in the class used to make me feel even worse. They used to make fun of me and say I was stupid because I couldn't tell the time and had messy handwriting.' Rachel's mum gave her a hug. 'We then decided to find out what was causing your problems with reading and writing,' her mum said. 'That's when things began to get much better.'

▸ Rachel remembers being bullied because of her dyslexia. There were times when she didn't want to go to school.

DYSLEXIA FACTS

Detection

It is likely that in every class of schoolchildren, one child will be dyslexic. Dyslexia affects people regardless of their background and has nothing to do with low intelligence. In fact, dyslexia is easier to detect in people who are very clever. Several GENIUSES have been dyslexic, such as the painter and inventor Leonardo da Vinci and the scientist Albert Einstein.

▲ Albert Einstein was a scientist who was awarded the Nobel Prize in 1921.

What is dyslexia?

I like going to Rachel's house because Rachel always thinks of fun things to do. We talk about lots of things, too. One day when she was upset after school, she told me that when she looks at a page of words, the letters seem to jump around. 'They won't keep still!' Rachel told me. 'Sometimes it's like the words are bunched up together and they look really blurred as well.'

It's weird that Rachel has trouble with reading and writing because she can do lots of other things really well. She's brilliant at following the diagrams you get in model kits and she's built some amazing things. She just seems to know what to do straight away. If we're doing an experiment in a science lesson at school, Rachel comes up with lots of good ideas. She sometimes gets cross if she can't think of a word to explain what she means, but she usually gets the right answer.

◀ Opposite: Rachel's favourite subject at school is science, especially when the class does experiments.

▲ Rachel wishes she could read out loud without stopping or making mistakes.

DYSLEXIA FACTS

What does it mean?

The word 'dyslexia' comes from the Greek language and means 'difficulty with words'. Children who are dyslexic somehow struggle to learn to read and write even though they are intelligent. But there are lots of ways in which people can deal with their dyslexia. And, as well as difficulties, people who have dyslexia often have special abilities. They may be very imaginative, creative or musical, or good at acting or sport.

What causes dyslexia?

No one knows exactly what causes dyslexia, but experts think it has something to do with how the brain deals with the information it receives. The brains of dyslexic people aren't damaged, they may just work differently from the brains of non-dyslexic people. The brain is the control centre for the whole body. It may look like a wrinkled grey sponge, but it is more complicated than the most powerful computer. In an adult, the brain weighs about 1kg. Most of this weight is due to a part of the brain called the CEREBRUM.

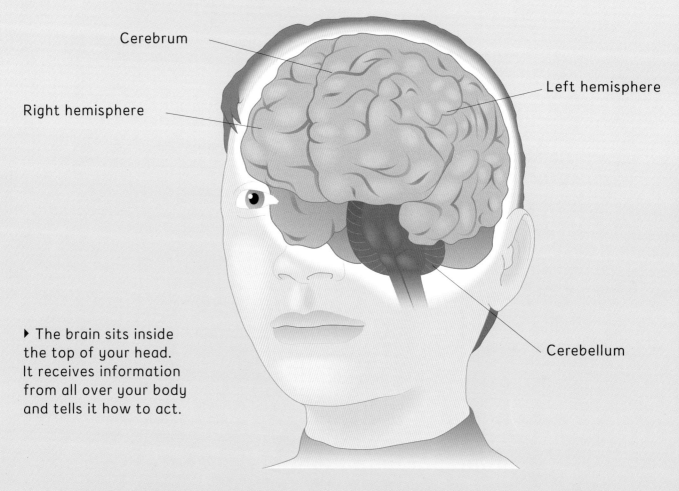

Cerebrum

Right hemisphere

Left hemisphere

Cerebellum

▶ The brain sits inside the top of your head. It receives information from all over your body and tells it how to act.

The cerebrum is split into two halves, which are known as the left and right HEMISPHERES. Some scientists think that each hemisphere deals with different body functions. They suggest that the right hemisphere helps us to think about things as whole pictures rather than as separate parts of a picture. It controls creative thought and allows us to visualise things like colours, patterns and shapes.

The left hemisphere is thought to look after things such as speech, words, maths, sequences and sounds. Scientists think that people with dyslexia may think more with the right hemisphere than the left, which might explain why dyslexic people have problems with reading and writing but are often very talented in areas such as art, design and music.

New scientific research has shown that a part of the brain called the CEREBELLUM may also have something to do with dyslexia. It controls how the body moves and balances and some scientists now think that the cerebellum is also involved in how humans learn.

▲ Dyslexia often runs in families. So if a child is dyslexic it is likely that someone else in the family, such as a father or grandmother, will be dyslexic too.

Diagnosing dyslexia

▶ Mr Kent is an educational psychologist. He has studied how children learn and advises them on how to make the most of their abilities.

'Mum, what made you decide to find out whether I had dyslexia?' Rachel asked. Her mum answered: 'I could see you were unhappy at school so I went to talk to your teacher. She said she could see that you were clever, but that you were getting frustrated with reading and writing because you were finding it harder than others in the class. She showed me some of the work you'd been doing and told me about the sorts of difficulties you'd been having.'

Rachel's mum made an appointment for Rachel to see an EDUCATIONAL PSYCHOLOGIST called Mr Kent. Rachel said: 'Mr Kent was very friendly. He gave me lots of tests to do, but they weren't like tests at school – I enjoyed them. In one test I had to look at some pictures and spot the mistakes in each one.'

Afterwards Mr Kent talked to Rachel and her mum. He explained that the results of the tests showed that Rachel was very clever and that she was dyslexic.

▸ Mr Kent gave Rachel both written and spoken tests to do.

DYSLEXIA FACTS

Dyslexic difficulties

Some difficulties that children with dyslexia may have include:

- forgetting things they have just been asked to do (even though they can remember things that happened a long time ago)
- finding it hard to break down words into individual sounds, for example, 'd-r-u-m'
- getting numbers and letters the wrong way around, such as reading '36' as '63' or mixing up 'b's' and 'd's'
- getting left and right or up and down confused
- finding it hard to list days of the week or months of the year in order

Visiting Rachel's grandma

Sometimes Rachel takes me to visit her grandma. I like going to her house because she's always pleased to see us. Rachel's grandma asks us lots of questions about what's happening at school. She says things were different when she was at school. 'Looking back, I think I must have been dyslexic just like Rachel,' she said, 'but few people knew about dyslexia when I was a child. I struggled with spelling and the teachers used to tell me off. I can smile about it now, but at the time it made me very sad.'

'When I went to see Mr Kent he asked Mum if anyone in the family has dyslexia,' Rachel remembered. 'I didn't think you could be dyslexic because you're always reading, and you used to make up fantastic stories.'

'Well, being dyslexic doesn't have to stop you from doing anything,' said Rachel's grandma. 'These days there are lots of ways to help with spelling. I use the spellchecker on my computer when I'm writing letters. I wish there'd been computers when I was growing up!'

◄ Opposite: Rachel and Bella enjoy visiting Rachel's grandma.

▲ Rachel's grandma thinks she is probably dyslexic like Rachel.

DYSLEXIA FACTS

Dyslexic Talents

Some talents that children with dyslexia may have include:
- having a strong visual sense and being good at designing, drawing or painting
- being skilled with their hands and good at sculpting or model-making
- having vivid imaginations and being able to create fantastic ideas and stories
- having practical skills, such as being able to work out how to use equipment

At school

▶ Miss Abbott is very happy with the way that Rachel's school work has improved.

Rachel said that Mr Kent told her to remember three things: that she's clever; that it's not her fault she's dyslexic; and that there are lots of things she can do to help her deal with her dyslexia. He wrote a report about all the tests he'd done with Rachel. In the report Mr Kent made a list of things that could be done to help Rachel at school. He said that sometimes Rachel could tell someone what she wants to say for that person to write down, so Rachel can concentrate on her ideas without worrying about her spelling. Rachel's mum gave the report to our

▸ Rachel enjoys school and feels much more confident since finding out that she is dyslexic and how to deal with it.

teacher, Miss Abbott, so she would know how to help. Now, if Miss Abbott wants us to remember something, like bringing in a permission letter for a school trip, she writes it down for Rachel to remind her. I can help too. Rachel sometimes phones me if she's forgotten what homework we have to do.

DYSLEXIA FACTS

Helping with dyslexia

Some things that children have found helpful in dealing with their dyslexia include:

- having coloured paper rather than white to write on which reduces the glare from the writing surface, so that the words aren't as hard to see
- using coloured OVERLAYS that they can put over the page of a book to change its colour
- wearing glasses with tinted lenses
- reading books that use a TYPEFACE that has been specially designed to help people with dyslexia, such as this book you are reading now

After school

Every Wednesday after school, Rachel goes to see Mr Pearson.
Mr Pearson is giving Rachel extra lessons to help her with writing and
spelling. I usually go with Rachel's mum to pick Rachel up because we
have a swimming lesson together afterwards. Rachel says the lessons
with Mr Pearson are fun because she uses her eyes, ears and her hands
to help her learn things.

'When I'm learning how to spell a new word,' she says, 'I practise the movement my hand makes when I write it. Then I can remember how to spell the word by remembering the movement.'

Mr Pearson isn't like a teacher at school. At the end of the lesson he lets Rachel choose a game for them to play together. Rachel's favourite is when they play snap with letter sounds – even when she doesn't win!

◄ Opposite: Mr Pearson shows Rachel how she can use her different senses to help her learn.

▲ Rachel and Mr Pearson finish their lessons with a game that encourages quick thinking.

DYSLEXIA FACTS

Learning with the senses

MULTI-SENSORY LEARNING is a way of learning that involves a combination of the body's senses, such as hearing, sight and touch. Here are some ways in which it can help children with dyslexia:

- drawing a simple picture, called a 'mind map'. This can help to plan a story or collect information for a project
- recording stories on tape and playing them back makes writing less pressured
- telling a story to someone to write down helps dyslexic children to focus on what they want to say
- drawing letters in a tray of sand can help children to remember the movement needed to write that letter

Computer club

▶ Learning to touch-type has helped Rachel to deal with her dyslexia.

On Thursdays Rachel goes to a computer club. She is using a special computer programme that is teaching her to touch-type. That means she can type without having to look at the keyboard. Rachel's been learning touch-typing for a year now, and she can now type really quickly. She knows where each letter is on the keyboard without having to think about it. It makes me laugh when I watch her type and see the words appearing on the screen – it's like magic!

▸ Rachel often types up her homework on her computer at home.

Rachel says that being able to type is another way of dealing with her dyslexia. When we have something like a story or a science investigation to write for homework, Miss Abbott lets Rachel type hers on the computer.

Typing is much quicker than writing something by hand, so her homework does not take as long as it used to. Rachel says she also uses the computer to design her work so that it looks good.

DYSLEXIA FACTS

Computer programmes

There are many computer programmes that can help children with dyslexia. Some offer spelling games that help children to learn spelling rules and patterns. Others show children how they can organise their ideas into a piece of writing. A spellchecker on a computer tells children if they need to correct a word they have misspelled. Some programmes read back what someone has written, so children can hear the words they have typed.

Weekend sleepover

Rachel and I love having sleepovers at each other's houses. When I go to Rachel's, her mum gets a Chinese take away and we all share it. Spring rolls are my favourite and Rachel loves noodles with bean sprouts. We always have to stop Rachel's brother Sam from taking too many spring rolls! I like Sam – he makes me laugh. Rachel says he's really annoying! I think they get on well with each other though. Before Rachel was diagnosed with dyslexia, she used to get upset a lot because she didn't

▶ Bella and Rachel like listening to a story at bedtime.

◀ Opposite: Rachel's brother Sam used to get upset because Rachel was given more attention than he was because of her dyslexia.

like going to school. Sam used to get a bit jealous because Rachel got a lot of their mum's attention. Things are fine now that Rachel is happier. She is getting help with her dyslexia and this has made a big difference to her.

Before we go to sleep at night, we listen to a story or some music on Rachel's CD player. Sometimes, Rachel's mum says, we fall asleep before it has finished playing!

DYSLEXIA FACTS

Audio learning

Recordings on tape or CD can help children with dyslexia, especially if they find it easier to remember the things they have heard. Some children find that it helps them to learn things such as times tables in maths if they record them and then play them back.

Having fun

▶ Rachel practises for the gymnastic display.

I like spending time with Rachel. We enjoy doing the same sorts of things, like shopping for clothes or going to the cinema. We both like gymnastics, too. I like doing cartwheels and Rachel is best at handstands. Next month we are both taking part in a gymnastic display at school, so we are practising hard for that. I've been in one before, but it's Rachel's first time. She didn't feel she was good enough before, even though our teacher said she would be fine. Since Rachel has had help with her dyslexia it has made her far more confident about everything she does. 'I used to feel that I was stupid and that people would laugh at me,' she says 'now I know that I'm dyslexic I feel better because there are lots of things I can do to deal with it.'

We both like entering fun competitions in magazines. Once we had to design a poster for a wildlife park. Rachel's design won a prize. I was a bit jealous at first, but Rachel won two tickets to visit the park, so we went together!

▲ Rachel is very artistic and she enjoys creating pictures and posters with Bella.

DYSLEXIA FACTS

Famous Dyslexics

Dyslexia is no barrier to achievement. Famous people with dyslexia have shown their talents in many areas such as:

- ACTING Salma Hayek
- ARCHITECTURE Lord Richard Rogers
- COOKING Jamie Oliver
- FASHION DESIGN Tommy Hilfiger
- PAINTING Leonardo da Vinci
- POLITICS Winston Churchill
- SCIENCE Thomas Edison
- SCULPTURE Auguste Rodin
- SINGING Cher, Robbie Williams

Questions people ask

Q. Who gets dyslexia?
A. Dyslexia is not an illness like measles or a cold that you can catch. No one is sure exactly what causes it, but it has been diagnosed in people whose brains work in a certain way (see pages 12 and 13).

Q. Is there a cure for dyslexia?
A. Dyslexia is not an illness, so there is no 'cure' for it. However, scientists and people involved in education know a lot about how dyslexia affects people and how to help them. There are many ways in which people who have dyslexia can work hard to improve their reading and writing skills.

▲ Magnetic letters can be used as a simple teaching aid in the home.

▲ Rachel has now learned many ways to help her deal with being dyslexic.

Q. How can I tell if I am dyslexic?
A. There are several pointers that suggest whether someone might be dyslexic. The symptoms vary greatly from person to person, but may include forgetting things easily, getting numbers or letters the wrong way around, spelling the same word differently at each attempt, finding it difficult to remember lists of things (such as the months of the year) in the correct order and having difficulty

telling the time. If you think you may be dyslexic, talk to an adult at home or at school. You may be able to visit an educational psychologist who will be able to test whether you are dyslexic.

Q. What's it like to be dyslexic?
A. Many dyslexic people say they get very frustrated by their problems with reading and writing. It can be lonely to feel different from others who don't share the same problems. Sometimes they have trouble organising their thoughts or thinking of a quick answer, and this makes them feel left out when they are in class or with their friends. People feel better when they know what they can do to deal with their dyslexia. Some people look on dyslexia as a gift, because they are often talented in other areas.

Q. How can I help my friend who is dyslexic?
A. Just treat them the same as you treat everyone else! It is also useful for someone who is dyslexic to be able to ask a friend for help if they have forgotten something, such as what they are meant to be doing for homework or bringing into school the next day.

Q. Are there any jobs that dyslexic people cannot do?
A. No! Dyslexia needn't stop someone from doing anything they want to do. Many great leaders, scientists, writers and inventors have been dyslexic, and there are people with dyslexia all over the world enjoying their lives and being successful in the careers they have chosen.

▸ Many famous people have learned how to cope with dyslexia; for instance, the politician and wartime leader Sir Winston Churchill was dyslexic.

Glossary

CEREBELLUM A part of the brain that lies underneath the cerebrum and controls how the body moves and balances. Some scientists think it is also involved in how people learn.

CEREBRUM The part of the brain that takes up most of its weight and that allows human beings to think.

DIAGNOSIS The identification by a qualified person of a problem such as dyslexia by considering someone's symptoms and the results of tests.

DYSLEXIA When someone of 'normal' intelligence has difficulty with reading, writing and spelling. These difficulties may be combined with abilities in other areas; for instance, people with dyslexia are often very creative or inventive.

EDUCATIONAL PSYCHOLOGIST Someone who has studied how children learn and can help children who are having difficulty with their schoolwork.

GENIUS Someone with extraordinary ability in a certain area, such as music, maths, science, art or language.

HEMISPHERES The right and left halves of the cerebrum in the brain.

MULTI-SENSORY LEARNING A way of learning that uses a combination of the body's senses, for example, seeing a letter, hearing how it sounds when it is read aloud, feeling the 3-D shape of the letter (such as a plastic fridge magnet) and experiencing the movement needed to write it.

OVERLAY A sheet of see-through coloured film that is placed over a page of writing to change the background colour of the page, for example, from white to yellow.

SYMPTOMS The ways in which someone shows that they may have a particular problem or illness; for instance, coughs, sneezes and a sore throat are symptoms of a cold.

TYPEFACE The shape and style used for the letters in a piece of printed writing.

Useful organisations

HERE ARE SOME ORGANISATIONS YOU MIGHT LIKE TO CONTACT
FOR MORE INFORMATION ABOUT DYSLEXIA

AFASIC
2nd Floor
50–52 Great Sutton Street
London EC1V 0DJ
Tel: 020 7490 9410
info@afasic.org.uk
www.afasic.org.uk
Helpline: 0845 3555577

BRITISH DYSLEXIA ASSOCIATION
98 London Road
Reading
Berkshire RG1 5AU
Tel: 0118 966 2677
Helpline: 0118 966 8271
E-mail: helpline@bda-dyslexia.demon.co.uk
www.bda-dyslexia.org.uk

BRITISH DYSLEXICS
www.dyslexia.uk.com

THE DYSLEXIA INSTITUTE:
National training and resource centre
Park House, Wick Road
Egham
Surrey TW20 OHH
Tel: 01784 222300

Fax: 01784 222333
www.dyslexia-inst.org.uk

THE DYSLEXIA RESEARCH TRUST
65 Kingston Road
Oxford OX2 6RJ
www.dyslexic.org.uk

National Literacy Trust
www.literacytrust.org.uk

OTHER WEBSITES
www.iamdyslexic.com
Not an organisation, but a very useful
website, run by teenager
Barnaby Blackburn. On the site,
Barnaby explains how he deals with
his dyslexia and gives useful tips about
how people and products can help
someone who is dyslexic.

Index